Bee Stings And Afterthoughts

Bee Stings And Afterthoughts

❧

MUSINGS AROUND REMOVING THE STINGER

By Cary Bright

Sticks Stones And Silver Linings

Contents

Dedication	vii
Some Days, Most Days	1
Anchovies	2
Buried In Dirt	3
The Crow	4
Bee Stings And Afterthoughts	5
Ellen	6
Burned	7
Dark Imaginings	8
Duality	9
Dinero	10
Seedlings	11
Tender Heart Bear	12
The Blues	14
Dishes	15
Devoured	16
In A Heap	17
Sad Eyes	18

Phantom 19

Thought Break 20

Wo-Moon 21

Dearly Departed 22

Meteor 24

Song Break - Sung To The Tune Of My Favorite Things 25

Peachy Keen 26

Tea 27

Lightning 28

Illusionary Heart 29

How We Rise 30

Body Work 32

Pisces Full Moon 33

Queen Of Daydreams 34

Tori 35

Nothing Is Wrong 36

Shells 38

Self-Loathing, A Cycle 39

When I Die 40

Blessings Are For Counting 42

About The Author 43

For husband and son.
Thank you for being Beebalm.

Some Days, Most Days

Some days I'm sure of what I want,
Most days I don't think I'll ever get there.
Some days I'm eager to "do,"
Most days my spunk wanes before I can.
Some days there's a fire lit under my ass,
Most days the flames fizzle before the roar even begins.
Some days I want to get out there and explore,
Most days fatigue gets the best of me and exploration is confined to
my thoughts.
Some days I read three chapters, flipping pages with vigor,
Most days my book remains unopen, its story unheard.
Some days inspiration comes easy,
Most days I must wade thru swampy waters to find it.
Some days I don't care that most days I'm unhinged,
Most days I'm anchored to what some day might bring.

Anchovies

My favorite singer refers to herself as anchovies, because not everyone likes those hairy little things.

I know that I am anchovies.

I am aware of how much joy my presence does not evoke.

My conversation is shallow, except when it's not.

When it's not, it's as deep as the ocean, and anglerfish lurk.

My Theia lies dormant to my Nyx who guides the way.

I'm conscious of my face and the bold language it speaks.

My gait is not soft, and my energy enters the room fiercely.

I talk to myself without moving my lips, so I'm usually in deep conversation.

My aloofness is not intentional, I'm just wrapped up in thoughts.

Swirling thoughts, jumbled, and disordered.

Buried In Dirt

I take a deep breath in, a deeper breath out. Lilacs. That smell is unmistakable.

Hurriedly my hands move through the leaves, I know I buried it here.

I had dug a hole only 4 inches deep and about 6 inches wide to fit it in.

My fingernails left muddied from earth that wasn't soft enough.

My fingers cut by rocks and roots whose home I have disturbed in my quest.

My blood lending itself to rebirth.

My dedication to the search and seizure of this thing that I have left behind is strong and unrelenting.

I know that I buried a piece of brokenness under a tree that drips sap in the summertime and leaves its hardened resin on cars parked in the driveway.

A tree whose leaves become crispy and withered and fall on top of holes that have been dug.

Whose shade drapes itself over broken girls who bury pieces of themselves in the dirt.

The Crow

Truth be told you could count the crows, sure as the wind blows, and trees grow.

They are steady. Their caw loud. Their feathers dark as night.

They hover above my house and take flight from my tree's limb.

Earbuds in snug, music loud in my ears, I'm intent on walking these shoes straight through my fears.

He stops six feet away (he knows the rules). I knew he was male.

I said, "hello!" His eyes met mine, and he had me.

I wonder if he thinks I'm like the others. I assure him I'm not.

We look into each other's eyes, mine are bloodshot.

He didn't wince, didn't "Caw!" just cocked his head to the side.

"Okay," I say, "hope to see you again!" and I continue my stride.

One moment in time, I locked eyes with a Crow.

His eyes met mine.

His eyes let me go.

I don't speak Crow, but I know for certain that my fine feathered friend had come to rescue me.

Bee Stings And Afterthoughts

Swollen lumps and eyelids
Bruised skin and egos
Bee stings and afterthoughts
Words wrought with anger.

Madness bound to fists.
Promises of better times.
Broken hearts and fat lips
Dried tears on rosy cheeks.

Scratched faces and shattered glass
Torn papers and glaring eyes
Gifts offered as a sign of peace.
One more day in a broken home.

Ellen

She stands by clutching her stuffed unicorn as her mom and dad scream at each other. As hands fly in the air and land on their intended target, she stands by nervously fumbling her tiny fingers through the mane of her toy companion. Their loud voices and flailing hands do not know their power when they fall on her young ears. They leave stains on her 8-year-old memory, cementing her insecurity. A foundation of chaos lays its building blocks down, marrying her to instability. The fear in her eye's brims at her lids and spills down her cheeks, she buries her face in the magic of the fluffy animal in her arms. In one second, she is taken away from her reality, and off to the mystical land where unicorns play, and fairy's dance. A place where she can hide among the mushrooms as frogs hop from lily pad to lily pad. She silences out the screams and immerses herself in a different dimension. Leaving the screaming scenery, she is welcome on her unicorn among soft moss and the long limbs of weeping willows. Her unicorn's white hair is soft under her cheek, resting here she closes her eyes, and wishes to make this her home.

Burned

She's a beautiful dark-haired woman, her stature small and meek.
He towers over her, the smell of liquor wafting from his breath.
A rage takes him over as he spits accusations in her direction, spraying spit in her face as he seethes.
She pleads the truth to deaf ears, and the spirits on his breath light a flame on the stove.
He grows twice in size; she shrivels, cowering beneath him.
His fury comes down like thunder and he grabs her hand placing it over the flame.
Like a woman at the stake, pulling away and saving herself will condemn her spirit.
Allowing her hand to char will clear her name.
Her devotion to him hangs in the balance.
How long can she tolerate the searing of her flesh?
Her skin cooks like the day's meal as she withstands a torture dealt by the man of the house.
She cries out in pain, and he basks in it.
His fury and her fear dance around the open flame.
He releases her and she writhes in pain, clutching her scorched hand.
Still branded a whore.

Dark Imaginings

I've spent my share of time with dark imaginings,
Lost myself in the anxiety and the webs that they bring.
Made up scenarios of "never going to happens,"
Leave me dreading the day and the shape that I'm left in.
A sliding scale of thoughts invade my mind, my brain plays the meanest of tricks,
I rock back and forth, shake my knee like a leaf, finding comfort in my ticks.
The horrors of my mind bind me up like a cocoon,
So I weigh myself down with blankets, and find a cat to spoon.
Curled up tightly, fighting to avoid the murky swamp,
While the imaginings lace up their boots, headed to my heart to stomp.
I'm barely hanging on, having braced myself on a ledge,
Anticipating the tipping point that will take me over the edge.
They dangle themselves like carrots, just hanging out taking up space,
Leaving my body paralyzed, frozen in place.

Duality

Wedged between delirium and reality.
A line so fine its erasure is a certainty.
She lives here, in this vat of quandary.
A mix of "I'm enough" and inadequacy.
Her mind scatters so easily.
Remnants left behind; she gathers them eagerly.
Teeter then totter always searching for stability,
It ain't easy to find in this mental infirmary.
Seeking and finding that it's out of proximity.
Sinking down deeper under the weight of this gravity.
Covering up the breadcrumbs maintaining obscurity,
Digging down deep to muster sincerity.
Holding on tight to fight off complicity,
Trying to vibe to a much higher frequency.
Losing touch, she is fighting calamity,
Exposing her scars, lacking timidity,
She opens herself up to the rest of humanity.
Discarded and forsaken out of vicinity,
She holes herself up, wrapped up and solitary.
Closing her eyes, she prays for vitality,
One more chance to find her divinity.
Struggling, she fumbles through this duality.

Dinero

Tides in and tides out, the smell of salty air, dead fish, and tanning oil.
Fishermen with high hopes of this evening's seafood boil.
Sand between my toes driving me batty as a loon,
It's like a mirror for the sky the way the ocean reflects the moon.
We walk up with our drums tucked under our arms, excited as could be.
2 little girls on spring break wanting to bang our drums with glee.
We laughed so hard as we walked up over the hill,
Only to find the tide had come in, our sandy beach swallowed up like a pill.
On our way back to our room we giggled and sang,
Voices on high, I the Yin, and she my Yang.
Nomads we were in our days of youth,
Without her, I'd have never left home, and that's the truth.
We let each other just be exactly the way we were.
She never tried to change me. Who could ever change her?
That first trip together, Myrtle Beach with not a parent!
Lead to many more, our love for each other inherent.
Tides in and tides out, we came and went from each other through life,
No matter how long, or how far, it was always just a matter of time.
We'd make our way back, we'd settle into our roles again,
Until we couldn't exist on this plane together as friends.
I look up at that Moon, and know she is out there beyond.
The Yang to my Yin, death could never break our bond.

Seedlings

The wind blows the seedlings of flowers whose petals have shriveled up and takes with it all the strength she had mustered up. As quick as it came, it was all gone again. Back to square one. She plants new seeds. She sows them down deep and carries a hoe along the way. Just a little baby sprout looking for something to lean on, to hold her up until she finds her footing. She peeks out from the dirt and sees the light. The warmth, enough to pull her out. She is showered in it, takes it all in and holds it tight. "This will do for now." She tells herself. Just enough for today. As she grows stronger, her scent is alluring and those who want some take a sniff. Some take a petal, and others pluck her from her root. Maybe she'll shrivel up on their dashboard, her petal dust blowing onto the highway on long drives.

Tender Heart Bear

The most tender-hearted woman I know calls me her
Tender Heart Bear.

Render the word tender down to its most slender form,
whatever that may be, its softness will still glide off your tongue.
The way her love glides out onto all her babies, babies' babies,
and those babies' babies' babies.

A mender she is, this tender-hearted soul, she'll patch you up,
and make you whole.

A lender as well, you need it? She's got it, and if she doesn't, she'll get it.

A bender of rules for those she holds so dear,
no rule is written in gold, so have no fear.

A defender, too, she'll fight anyone off who crosses her pack,
she'll bare her teeth, she'll gnash and bite back.

A sender of love, and goodies made from the heart,
good wishes, good food, good times if, of her life, you're a part.

Emotional, watery and intuitive, the four chambers of this
tender Pisces heart, is overflowing with love, wisdom,
and courage to impart.

If you know her, you're lucky. If she loves you, you're luckier.
She'll wrap you up, and hold you tightly, until you feel secure.

Her tender knows no bounds, her heart not held to only one.
She'll take you in, do all these things and more,
her tender won't come undone.

The Blues

Best get under the blankets because the blues are setting in. Navy, Indigo, Royal, those Blues not the Turquoise of the sky, or the Periwinkle that I love. The kind that are heavy and make my stomach flutter. The ones that won't let up until they are way beyond the pale. Those blues that leave the illusion that they are stronger than the Yellows, stronger than the Reds, and leave you scratching under the Pink. Blues before Orange, or Purples for that matter. They take over out of nowhere and slip in sly like the Greens of envy. Blues over Blacks, even the Blacks aren't this glum. They do their part and absorb, sucking it all in. Blues that make the Greys seem like a good time, at least they sometimes turn White, but Blue is as Blue comes in, and Blue stays until he's had enough.

Dishes

It might sound crazy but I find peace in doing dishes. I've never owned a dishwasher in my adult life, and there isn't really room for one in my kitchen. There isn't really room for one in my heart. I've cried over sinks full of dishes and my tears cleansed them as they cleansed my soul. I've taken frustration out on the grime stuck to pans like old wounds, hoping that by scrubbing the grime, I can remove what's been left gaping. At times dish soap makes my hands slippery, and my clumsiness is no match. Many a glass has perished by my hand leaving shards behind. I look through clear water for clear glass like looking for pieces of myself in the bottom of the basin, careful not to cut myself on memories too painful, their sharpness can still cut so deep. I've stood hell bent over that sink trying to wash away that brown stain that lingers on white bowls and dishes. I try bleach to remove it, but to no avail, it's left its stain there for everyone to see. New friends and old, new family, or old, one look at those lingering stains and it's easy to see that life has been at the bottom of that bowl. My personalization of such ware may seem bizarre to some. It's as if I can't part with it, we've so many times together, how I could simply toss this Santa's Cookies plate? Santa has been cradled by the hands of a toddler, then a little boy, then a teenager...Santa is now part of the family. No dishwasher will you ever find in my home. My head, hands, and heart need to do dishes.

Devoured

Low flying aircraft sprays **doom** across the sky, cutting the heads off
flowers.
The engine devours them using their stems like toothpicks.
The humming Cessna drowns out her cries, her bellows

       lost

          in

            flight.

In A Heap

At my most vulnerable point in life I was distilled down to a heap on my mother's couch. The distorted thoughts in my head were as heavy as a led blanket. The tears I was crying could fill a small pool and left my head thumping and cloudy. I was digging down to the depths of my soul to lift from underneath the canopy of darkness that draped my fragile state. You could've huffed, puffed, and blown me down to a pile of rubble with one slight breath, and I would've stayed there. The effort it took to come back from the blow was immense. I crawled, I clawed, I scratched, and dug my way to the surface. Day by day, breath by breath, light appeared. It was mine. And though it had dimmed for what felt like a lifetime, it had never burned out. It was that strong, and it was inside me, waiting.

Waiting for me to remember...

No blanket, no matter how heavy,

No canopy, no matter how dark could ever burn out my light.

And when I stand in my power, I am radiant. And I shine fiercely.

Sad Eyes

"No one grieves if they don't live and love." The words are inked on my rib cage, in memory of.

The pain I felt when she passed was excruciating, but it was no match to her last 8 months. She floated like a butterfly, and stung like a bee, but ultimately the fight was called.

I flinch as the needle rips open my flesh, it's as if I could hear my skin tearing. I welcome the physical pain which is no match for what my heart feels.

"Sad eyes, you knew there'd come a day, when we would have to say goodbye..." just one of "our" songs. The kind she would sing with me as she sat me up on the kitchen counter. My eyes were sad. My heart was sad. My ribs are burning, and my skin is dripping with blood.

I would have offered my pulse and my breath if we could have shared them. In that moment, her breathing was getting shallow, and each breath in was followed by silence.....until one more breath out. The time in between each was filled with tension, sadness, anticipation, and then relief as she took one more. Then it began again, tension, sadness, anticipation, exhale. Until it didn't come. And when it didn't come, we took off her gloves, wiped her down, and let her go.

My ribs are wiped down with green soap, the ointment is applied, and I'm sealed with dressing. My eyes are still sad. My heart is still sad. My ribs ache, but I am high on adrenaline. One moment of release so I could exhale.

Phantom

It's the flip flop after the first wear of the season between your toes when you're barefoot in bed.

It's the roller coaster ride on your way home from the amusement park.

It's the waves of the water after your body has been dry for hours.

It's the tingle in your body long after the orgasm has left you breathless.

It's the rocking in your body after the boat has docked and you've stepped on dry land.

It's the cast after your ankle's sprain has returned to its healed state.

The phantom is what you feel long after the thrill of the ride, the removal of the appendage,

the relief after the restriction.

The shadow.

The peace.

It hovers in wait...

Thought Break

I can't see the forest for the trees,

but I can see the hive for the bees.

Wo-Moon

I think of the moon, and myself.
The Moon and I.
Wo-Moon.

I wonder if she thinks of me, too. Does the Moon wonder at the 14th day why I've gone dark? Will she put out her crystals and charge them under the energy that is me at the time I am at my fullest? Maybe she gazes down at me, lights a candle, and beholds all the power that I harness. My magic, a yearning for her to be a part of as she feels the swells of the tides within her because I am shining, round and robust. I wonder what intentions she sets and declares when she holds ceremony simply because I am halfway to being.

Because I do...

I believe she's gone dark because even she needs a night to go far in. My crystals set under her glow to absorb her light and allow me the touch of softness and magnificence that feels far out of reach. The fire of my candle conjures up a special magic that works between she and I, and my flame dances of joy to be empowered by us girls.

She is shining, round and robust, and I am her reflection of a woman with the power to magnify.

Dearly Departed

His grief was on full display as he greeted everyone.

Her funeral came as a surprise to all who knew her.

His despair took center stage, moving those in attendance.

He couldn't hold back.

As they closed the lid to her casket he paced the room fervently, meeting the eyes of various people, making sure they knew she loved them.

In his grief, he found a way to hold others.

He made sure that everyone knew that she was being buried with his heart in her hand.

Tears streamed down his face, as he frantically tried to grasp what was happening.

His wife was leaving, too soon.

She was departing their life long before she was ready, and long before he was willing to let her go.

As if he ever could.

As long as he had breath in his body, she would never be forgotten.

He spoke of her and their love every day after she passed, and not a day went by that he didn't visit her grave.

He talked to her, and he played her music from the same radio that she played in her kitchen as she poured love into the three meals she cooked him each day.

He kept her up to date on family happenings, watching over her resting place with loving eyes.

He drove to the cemetery to be at her side until he could no longer get behind the wheel.

Patiently he waited, day to day, to join her, knowing that death was the only way his heart would ever be full again.

And when his day came, I couldn't help but find the happiness in their reunion.

Without her, his life wasn't the same.

Without him, she was still tethered to life.

In death, their hearts are joined, and they hold hands, they laugh, and they love, while patiently awaiting the rest of us.

Meteor

Memories flood like heavy rains and I return to the elevator where kisses linger.
In a dingy apartment building we began this trip by removing old stingers.
One by one, scanning for scars, drawing lines around them to be filled in.
Sutures made of promises, bandaids made of oaths peeled back and stuck to the skin.
There were others before, but really there were none,
Because our souls couldn't settle in the wrong constellation.
We touched down like a meteor, hitting hard and fast,
Shifting tectonic plates with our impact.
And like molten glass we fused together,
Particle by particle we were bound and tethered.
All tangled up in love and lust,
A belief in each other and hearts full of trust.
We dove into each other, right into the deep
Holding onto us with promises to keep.

Song Break - Sung To The Tune Of My Favorite Things

True crime tv shows with kitties on couches,
Knee high sock warmness, and crystals in pouches.
Warms cups of coffee, or cold brew at times,
These are some things that calm my anxious mind.
Blankets, and munchies, while scrolling through nonsense,
Keyless remote start, warm seats make me less tense.
Sunshine on snow is a beautiful sight,
These are some things that calm my anxious mind.
When my brain tries to take over, when I'm feeling sad,
I go through this list of things that I enjoy, and then I don't feel so bad.
Kettles of warm soup, with to many noodles,
Journals, and sketch books all filled with my doodles.
Books I get lost in with places to hide,
These are some things that calm my anxious mind.
Music and Yoga, and silence when needed,
Afternoons spent making things that are beaded.
Resting and sleeping when drained all the time,
These are some thing that calm my anxious mind.
When my brain tries to take over, when I'm feeling sad,
I go through this list of things that I enjoy, and then I don't feel
so bad.

Peachy Keen

It seems hard to write when things are peachy keen,
When my world's going right, my words seem so lean.
What am I if not dark, sad, and depressed?
Am I void of depth when I'm not swarmed with stress?
It feels hollow without triggers, is this what being "healed" feels like?
Must I write about old wounds for the rest of my life?
A vat of dark creativity bubbles within the wells of melancholy,
One that exists differently in times that are jolly.
Am I playing with fire putting these words down on paper?
Afraid I'm invoking despair; I tucked this one away for later.
Still in one piece, I come back to revisit this spell,
If anxiety and anguish lurk, I can't quite tell.
I strip myself down, I dig deep for the muse,
She's in a club in New Orleans, though, listening to the blues.
I'll stand by and wait on her, maybe she'll bring me back a tune.
And I'll play it over and over again under a sweet, dark Moon.

Tea

The varieties of tea that have taken residence in my cupboard out-number the cups of tea I've drank in my life. I buy tea because tea makes me feel like I'm bettering myself. Like one day, I'll be one of those girls who curls up with a cup of tea and a book at night, one of those girls who has her shit together. She eats well, and by well, I don't mean in large quantity. I have the tea. I have green tea, white chocolate peppermint tea, java tea, dandelion tea, turmeric tea, white tea, peach tea, dessert teas, tea bags from Chinese food restaurants, regular ol' tea, and even a big, huge giant jar of raw honey to go with the tea. I don't like the taste of honey, but I try to. I buy the tea, but seldom do those bags find themselves swimming in a cup of piping hot water.

The tag of the tea bag drapes over the side of a tea mug (it's not a coffee mug if it holds tea) like a trophy. A girl could sew that tag onto a sash like a girl scout having mastered the consumption of the proper amount of tea in a day. Or better, having learned how to blend flowers to make their own delicious elixir.

A lot of my friend's drink tea. I love them. They are some of the best people I know. Maybe if I drank tea, I'd be one of the best people they know. Maybe I already am, even though I drink coffee.

Lightning

If I had listened to the lightning, nothing would have changed.
It crashed down hard in my dream, and when I woke up, I knew what
it meant.
And it meant it.
Its warning was bold, the way lightning is, and in nearly 20 years' time
it's done nothing gently.
No, in 20 years' time it's been battle after battle, attacks coming from
the low end.
Still, 20 years later, there's no end in sight.
It's dry lightning, capable of starting forest fires, family fires, and
unfriendly fires.

Not the fire of Pele.
Not the Dance of Kali.

This fire deserves no goddess' name.
It comes from an evil down in the depths and pits.
There's no reconstruction, only war-torn destruction.
Its strike is self-serving, vile, and ugly.
Had I listened to it 20 years ago when it came to me in my dreams, my
shield would've been
made of rubber.
And I would've surrounded myself with lightning rods.

Illusionary Heart

May that which is an illusion present itself so that my fears dissipate.
May that which presents itself be clear, and full of truth.
May that which causes me fear provide a light for my heart as it sees its way out.
May that which is truth be bold enough to show itself to those who need to hear it.
May those who need to hear it have the capacity to take it in.
May their ears be the funnel to the heart where the truth is gently placed.
May it emblazon this space and encase it in golden amulets and talisman.
May these amulets dangle delicately from all four chambers, decorating them in power.
May the power of the heart be tender, yet raucous.
May its needs be heard from shadow sides and valleys,
May it spew authentically, casting spells in all directions.
May it call out to the wandering and let their weary souls find rest.

How We Rise

What choice are we left with but to rise?
Lie on the ground with our heads buried?
Fall deeper, deeper, and deeper into an abyss?
Silently suffer and stifle the love we are full of?

Not us.
We are of the strongest on the Earth.
We are light workers.
We are not here to fester in gloom.

When we rise, the ashes left behind will sparkle like gold dust left of
golden embers.
Our wings will open stronger, and fuller than before.
The light shining sacred from our crowns will illuminate for miles
ahead.
We'll glide above the skyscrapers, raining love light down on the
weakened.
As we lift our brethren, our sisterhood is strengthened.

When we rise, we'll drop our defenses. We'll soften around the edges
to cradle the sharp vitriol we encounter.
We'll surrender our swords, sheaths, and shields and embrace the dark
to bring it to light.
Our sacrifice, one of great strength, reverence, and necessity.

When we rise, our ferocity will be a surprise hidden behind a shield of feathers, and thick hyde.
When met with fear, we'll soften with grace. Our assurance that we know better will be met by skeptics.

We work with shadows, we have seen fear, and rise the victor.
We drown by no hand; no force can keep us down.

We rise strong.

We rise fierce.

We rise anew.

Body Work

It's kindness reciprocated.
It's tender hands moving lovingly across a war-torn body.
A touch of kindness and love enveloping skin and muscle,
Her hands like a touch of grace here to meet your hurt and help it heal.
She is the pure embodiment of Mother Earth, nurturing,
soulful, and loving.
In her presence, I am held, my body honored and recognized for all
its strife and anguish.
A warm salve seeps into the crevices and pores from soft hands being
guided by intuition.
I don't know how she knows, and I don't question it.
Hers is a knowing never led astray, and always led by a
nudge from the Goddess.
She is a part of my journey.
She is a part of my heart.
I am whole when I am with her, and she is always with me.

Pisces Full Moon

Full moons like these get my gears moving slowly,
though their capacity to out-think the heart is quick.
Nothing is impersonal.

I wade through emotion thick as waist high swamps,
eager to stand on solid ground again.
Though I know.

My legs will wobble, my knees will buckle,
and my bones will creak with each step forward.
I'll get there.

Full moons like these have tides rising high, oceans within,
eclipse the edge and swallow it whole.
My sanity is drowning.

All this hard work, years of it, always on the brink of
getting yanked out from under me.
This feels like forever.

Pray darkness wanes on day 29, raise a glass to fading voices,
and toss a coin for the swell's descent.
I need release.

Queen Of Daydreams

When I'm 10 years old the world around me is small, and I'm stuck in a prison, shackled to chaotic days filled with name calling and hate fueled vitriol. My attempt to escape is desperately futile. I wake from the same dream in the same place, it's like Ground Hog's Day. I mull over my plans in great detail to find the holes in the plot. There are so many.

When I'm 10 years old I learn what anxiety is, but I don't know that's what they call it yet so I just say I'm scared. Scared of what, I'm asked. Freddy Krueger. No lie. That's what I said.

But Freddy's nails are no match for the words that tore through my skin. His terror inducing nightmares are fairytales compared to my reality. My plan is the same as Nancy's. If Nancy can take control of Freddy in her dreams, I can take control of my chaos with dreams.

When I'm 10 years old I start to live in my head. They call it dissociation, but I don't know that word yet, so I call it daydreaming. I stare off into space during class and I'm anywhere but there. I'm off trying to rule a world in any realm I can.

I'm the Queen of my daydreams. I have all the power. I bow to no one. I am pretty. I am cared for. And I am fine.

When I was 10 years old I was all those things, I just didn't know it yet.

Tori

Her red blazes like fire while she sings sonic hymns.
They pierce me.
Her sequins catch the light and I blink quickly,
Not wanting to miss a thing.
Blinded for a moment and quietly moved to tears.
Her voice.
Her voice.
Her voice reminds me that I have my own (blanket girls know).
She empowers me.
She moves me.
Her hands beat on the keys of the Bose and strike against its body,
Bringing another element to her passion.
Her shoes, always on point.
Her witch, ever present.
Singing for those whose cries can't be heard.
Her potions are an elixir that soothes a hoarse voice box,
And remind me to let it out.

Nothing Is Wrong

There is nothing wrong with me. At the core of me I am beautiful, I am strong, I am brave, I am courageous. I walk into fires never doubting that I will come out shining bright. The scars and burns I take out of fire only make me stronger.

There is nothing wrong with me. At the core of me I understand that I have faults, that I am a work in progress. My potential is limitless, and I can do anything that I dream of. With my heart in the right place, I can only steer straight.

There is nothing wrong with me. My heart is big, my mind is strong willed, and my hands work to heal. I am compassionate to those in need and help when I am able. I am strong enough to ask for help when I need it, and I know that I am worthy of help.

There is nothing wrong with me. I am unlearning patterns that have not served my best interest and working towards my greater good. Because I am of a peaceful mind and heart, my greater good is also what is good for the collective.

There is nothing wrong with me. I try my best, I demand things of myself physically, I am working on being patient with my shortcomings. When I fall, I get back up. When I am wrong, I learn a lesson. When I am tested, I practice a pause.

There is nothing wrong with me and I am bold enough to speak truth. My voice amplifies when I speak of things I love. My eyes sparkle bright when I'm engaged in enjoyment. My ears listen intentionally to the words of those around me. My mouth tastes the sweetness of the air. My body is elated when touched by hands that emanate love.

I radiate light. I radiate love. I connect with my inner goddess, my inner warriors, and I share this life with them. I am hopeful.

Shells

Shells stick up like shards of glass cutting through the walls. How they hold something so fragile with fierce confidence. Intact, all bottled up, borderline suffocating. Broken down. Feeling oozes out like lava. Shocked and shattered having fallen again. The King's horses and the King's men came to my side, try as they might, my armor was stronger. My pieces on display, the lava too hot to touch. I'll stay here, face down, but just for today.

Self-Loathing, A Cycle

Waking up on days where I just want to cry, hate who I see in the mirror, hate what I'm doing to my body, and hate what my body is doing to me.

I watch inspirational videos of people who are lifting weights, exercising, being active, eating well, smiling and mindful of who they are.

I can't even type this because I hate it.

When I Die

When I die, leave my body for the vultures and the hawks to fill their bellies on. Give me a sky funeral, lay me on warm ground, and let wildlife pick apart my flesh down to the bones. Feed my bones to the crows, as they dance a murderous dance of exaltation for the gifts you bestow upon them.

When I die, burn my body to a cinder. Distill it down to a pile of ash, hair, and bone remnants. My mound of remains a canvas. Blow me into molten glass, let me take shape in a transparent cylinder, or a vase to hold your lively flowers. Pour my dust into an urn or into a body of water. Release me into the air, and let me land amongst the trees, leaves, and vines. Mix me up in your pipe, and inhale me into your lungs, release me with your breath into vapor.

When I die, lay me in a boat surrounded by beautiful crystals, wearing rings of gold and silver, pearl beads strung with lace, and a coin in my pocket to insure my place in the afterlife. Send me off to sea and let the waters have their way with the fate of my empty vessel. Let me sink into the deep sea, if the swells deem it so, and rest among treasure left behind by pirate ships, and submarines sunk in battle.

When I die, feed me to the forest in a mushroom suit. As my body is devoured by spores, my soul will rest easy knowing that I am now food of the forest. Trees will revel in the delight of the yummy nutrients the fungi leave unto them as they purify the toxins in my body and feed it to their long-limbed friends.

Blessings Are For Counting

"When I'm worried and I can't sleep,
I count my blessings instead of sheep."
It worked for Ol' Blue Eyes, so why not for me?
When my mind's bogged down with past tragedies,
And old times bubble up and my eyes begin to weep,
I count the daily blessings and pass on the sheep.

I count my blessings and sometimes twice,
Because there's a host of good things that make life nice.
Love and laughter, sadness and strife,
Danger and excitement, sugar and spice.
I count on blessings the way others count on Christ.

Yes, I count my blessings and sometimes thrice,
Cuz waking up each day is a roll of the dice.
And I'll try to distill it down and make this more precise,
Life is worth living but you gotta hold on tight.

The ride gets bumpy, and the days feel long,
But the years run right past you, and next thing, they're gone.
Everything about life is valid,
And all the words you say are a ballad,
A prayer, a spell from my lips to your heart,
Count your blessings as each day departs.

I'm a writer, artist, Yoga teacher, Witch, and a host of other identities on any given day. I've strapped myself into this bumpy ride called life, holding on tight to the smoother days. I enjoy spending time with my people, and I'm lucky enough to have a lot of them. There isn't anything complex about me, except sometimes. I love cats. I'm a beast at the gym. I have a corporate job that pays the bills and doesn't make me want to jump off a cliff. All around, I live a great life.

Yoga in Downtown Cleveland
Stacy Candow